Twister Free

By Marc Preston

Illlustrated by Joanne Friar

    Spring brings bright sunshine to the Midwest, where my home is. But spring can also mean thunderstorms. Thunderstorms brew up quickly and can bring twisters too. These twirling funnel clouds can be dangerous.

One day last spring, Mom was planting the garden. I had just returned home from my baseball game. I gave Mom my postgame report and then went inside for a snack. That was in the morning when the sky was a deep blue. By midday, though, it had changed and became a gray mass of dark storm clouds.

Mom came inside. "Turn on the television or radio," she told my sister Jen. "Let's get some up-to-date weather information. I think a big storm is likely. Dark, gray clouds are racing across the sky, and the wind is blowing hard."

Jen clicked the remote. "Storm watch for Lake and Cook Counties," the reporter noted. Then he gave some good prestorm advice. "Seek shelter. Do not stay outside. Do not stand by windows. Do not be caught unprepared."

As we listened to the report, the rain began. At first, just drops fell, but then it came down in buckets and beat against the windows. Then I heard a loud wailing sound. "What was that?" I asked.

Mom explained, "It's the town's siren, which is sounded when there's a likelihood of a twister."

At school and home, we had learned about twisters. We knew we had to seek protection. The best place to find that was the basement. Jen and I didn't need much encouragement to move quickly. We knew the possible danger. We ran down and looked for a place to hide. Mom advised us to get under Dad's bench. "It's a good, solid piece of furniture," she said. "It will help protect us."

I scurried under it and Jen and Mom followed.
We huddled together. Windows began to rattle.
The noise got louder and louder. It sounded like a
train was speeding past the house. Jen whimpered.
I felt like crying too. But I tried to be brave. Mom
hugged us tightly. Then it was quiet.

Slowly we crept out and looked around the house. To our amazement, it was in perfect shape. We ran outside and looked up and down the road. Everything looked undamaged. Late afternoon news reports explained that conditions had been right for a twister but one never formed.

Since that day, we have paid close attention to storm watches. Mom said that last spring's storm was the only time she thought that we would have a twister. We are lucky. Our town has been free of twisters for as long as Mom can remember.